Instruments

Focus: Systems

PETER SLOAN &
SHERYL SLOAN

There are many types of
musical instruments.
Musical instruments make
different musical sounds.

A telescope is an instrument. It can make something that is far away appear very close. Telescopes are used to study the stars. Some telescopes are big and powerful and are kept in buildings called observatories.

A thermometer is an instrument. It measures temperature. A thermometer can be used to check if someone has a fever. Thermometers are also found on engines, ovens, and refrigerators.

A compass is an instrument.
It is used to find direction.
The points of a compass
show north, south, east,
and west. Ships and airplanes
use compasses to plot their
routes through the water and
the sky.

A speedometer is an instrument. It is used to measure speed. Speedometers are built into vehicles to show how quickly they are moving. Speedometers help drivers keep within the speed limit.

6

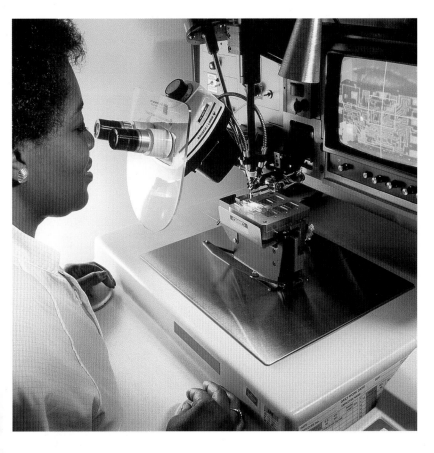

A microscope is an instrument. It can make something very small appear much larger. Microscopes are used in hospitals and laboratories to help doctors and scientists with research.

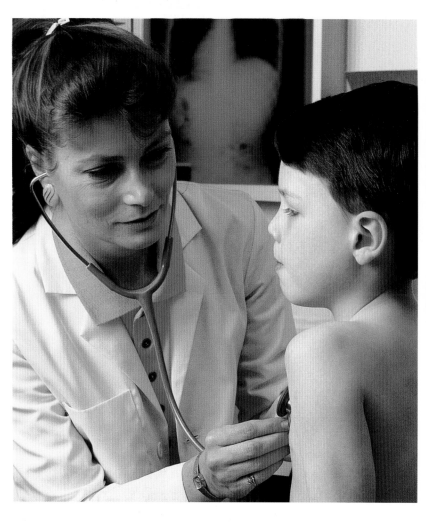

A stethoscope is an instrument.
It is used to hear sounds
inside the body. Doctors use
stethoscopes to listen to their
patients' hearts and lungs.